Just Shut Up

Shut Up

and DO IT!

7 STEPS TO **CONQUER** YOUR GOALS

BRIAN TRACY

simpletruths.com

Photo Credits: page 1, Malchev/Shutterstock, Krista Joy Johnson; page 8, Macrovector/Shutterstock; page 11, Fenton one/Shutterstock; page 13, Macrovector/Shutterstock; page 21, Spreadthesign/Shutterstock; page 27, Macrovector/Shutterstock; page 31, Macrovector/Shutterstock; page 35, Matthew Cole/Shutterstock; page 43, jorgen mcleman/Shutterstock; page 48, Macrovector/Shutterstock; page 59, Macrovector/Shutterstock; page 65, La1n/Shutterstock; page 77, morokey/Shutterstock; page 87, Jane Kelly/Shutterstock; page 99, Dacian G/Shutterstock; page 113, BluezAce/Shutterstock; page 119, Tarchyshnik Andrei/Shutterstock; page 131, Alexandr III/Shutterstock; page 141, Dacian G/Shutterstock

Published by Simple Truths, an imprint of Sourcebooks, Inc.
P.O. Box 4410, Naperville, Illinois 60567-4410
(630) 961-3900
Fax: (630) 961-2168
www.sourcebooks.com

Printed and bound in China.

QL 10 9 8 7 6 5 4 3 2 1

CONTENTS

INTRODUCTION

Winning Is for
WINNERS

> "Deep within man dwell those slumbering powers; powers that would astonish him, that he never dreamed of possessing; forces that would revolutionize his life if aroused and put into action."
>
> —*Orison Swett Marden*

You probably have more talent and ability than you could use in one hundred lifetimes. You have all the intelligence you need, right now, plus the ability to learn any subject you need to learn to achieve any goal you can set for yourself. There are no limits on what you can be, do, and have, except for the limits you place on your own mind.

THE BIG QUESTION

Many years ago I began asking the question, "Why is it that some people are more successful than others?"

The most important answer surprised me, as it surprises most people. It is simple. Your success is based on what you do, the results you get, and how quickly and efficiently you achieve those results.

It is not based on what you say, wish, hope, or intend to do at some time in the future. Success

Success is only based on what you are doing right now in this moment.

is only based on what you are doing right now in this moment. As Henry Ford said, "You can't build a reputation on what you're going to do."

We are living in the fastest moving, most turbulent, disruptive, and unpredictable time in all of human history. This kind of rapid change often causes people to become distracted, unsure, insecure, and demotivated. As a result they just slow down, sit around, and accomplish very little.

THE MOST VALUABLE ASSET

What is a company's most valuable asset? According to the Harvard Business School, it is its reputation. A company's most valuable asset is what people say about the company, and its products and services, to other customers or potential customers.

Because technology, information, and customer tastes are changing rapidly, products and services are changing faster than ever before. But reputation remains. In fact, it is everything. Think about companies like Apple and Google. Their reputations are so excellent that they are world leaders in the products and services they offer.

So, what is *your* most valuable asset? It is your reputation as well. It is what people think and say about you when you're not there. It is the words that people use to describe you and especially how well they think you do your work.

GETTING THINGS DONE

The most important part of your reputation is your ability to start and complete important tasks, to get things done, and to be known for speed and dependability. This will do more to make your happiness, health, success, and wealth than any other facet of your reputation that you can develop.

What is your main goal in life? According to Aristotle, behind every goal there is another goal until you finally reach the main goal, which is to be happy. Everything you do is an attempt, successful or not, to achieve happiness in some way. In fact, you can measure your level of success by what percentage

Everything you do is an attempt, successful or not, to achieve happiness in some way.

of time you are a genuinely happy person. This is more important than all the money and accomplishments in the world.

THE ACHIEVEMENT OF HAPPINESS

How do you achieve happiness? In its simplest terms, happiness is the progressive realization of a worthy goal or ideal. It is only when you feel that you are moving step by step toward the accomplishment of something that is important to you that you feel genuinely fulfilled and happy.

Everyone wants to be a "winner." They want to be seen and thought of as a winner by others. How do you achieve this? Simple— you win!

What is winning? In running when you cross the finish line before any of the other runners, you win.

In life you win when you start and complete your most important tasks on time and, ideally, before anyone else—you cross the finish line first. As a result you feel wonderful about yourself. Your brain releases endorphins, nature's "happy drug," which gives you an overall sense of peace and well-being. You feel like a winner.

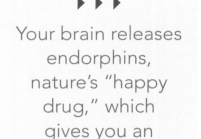

▶ ▶ ▶

Your brain releases endorphins, nature's "happy drug," which gives you an overall sense of peace and well-being.

GET STARTED AND KEEP GOING

In its simplest terms, your ability to get started and to keep going until you complete those things that are most important to you and to your company is the key to winning, to happiness, to a great reputation, and to success in life.

In the pages ahead, I will share with you a simple, practical, proven seven-part method to accomplish more in the next few months and years than most people accomplish in a lifetime.

LET'S BEGIN.

CHAPTER ONE

The Biggest Obstacle to
SUCCESS

> "We first make our habits, and
> then our habits make us."
> —*John Dryden*

Fully 95 percent of what you do, or fail to do, is determined by your habits. Your actions are determined by your habits of belief—the way you are programmed as a result of your lifetime of experience—and your habits of behavior—what you are accustomed to doing or not doing.

The biggest obstacle to success is that people have negative habits, sometimes unconsciously, that hold them back, year after year, from realizing their full potential.

The good news is that all habits, first of thought and then of behavior, are learned. Because your habits are learned, they can be unlearned, and replaced with new, positive, constructive habits that enable you to get going, keep going, and do great work that gets you paid more and promoted faster.

DEVELOP NEW, BETTER HABITS

Habits are developed by taking in new information that's either positive or negative for us and then repeating actions based on that information until actions become automatic. Once the habit is locked in you respond automatically, neither questioning nor explaining to yourself what you have decided to do.

The worst habits of all are based on your self-limiting beliefs. These are areas where you believe yourself to be limited in some way even though it may not be true. But as a result, you act as if it was true and it then becomes true for you. The old saying is, "You are not what you believe you are,

but what you believe, you are."

▶ ▶ ▶

"You are not what you believe you are, but what you believe, you are."

Challenge Your Beliefs

The starting point of greater success is for you to take some time to challenge the automatic assumptions you make that may be holding you back from success.

Some people believe they are lacking in intelligence because they didn't get good grades in school. Then they find out that some of the most successful people in the most complex industries also did poorly in school.

Some people are unsuccessful because they do not believe they are creative, self-disciplined, good time-managers, punctual, or capable of learning and applying new things. They say, "That's just the way I am." They actually think that this is a reason for not growing and improving.

The fact is that most self-limiting beliefs are not true. They are based on information that you have taken in; sometimes they come from the opinions or criticisms of others, sometimes from something as simple as reading your horoscope.

The Brake on Your Potential

The worst of all self-limiting beliefs is the fear of failure. This is the fear of loss, poverty, mistakes, or not achieving a goal that you have set for yourself. People who are preoccupied with the fear of failure continually look for reasons why something cannot be done, why it's a bad idea, or why they may lose their time and money. The fear of failure, like all fears, paralyzes behavior, clouds thinking, and causes a person to feel like the proverbial deer in headlights.

TAMING ELEPHANTS

In my seminars, I often ask, "How do you train an Indian elephant?" At one time, Indian elephants were the "battle tanks" of the Maharajas. Not only did they carry boxes of bowman and spear throwers on their backs, but they were also violent and aggressive, attacking the enemy and impaling them on their sharpened tusks. They were so terrifying and fearless that enemy armies would run away when they were confronted by these elephants.

Today, these same elephants are beasts of burden. They calmly and peacefully plow the fields, haul logs, do what their masters tell them to do, and then stand around quietly in their corrals, waiting for the next day and more work. They have completely lost their ferocity and their ability to strike fear into the heart of the enemy. How did this happen?

The Training Begins

When the elephant was a baby the owner would take the little elephant away from its mother and tie its leg with a strong rope to a post driven deep into the ground. The baby elephant would

They have completely lost their ferocity and their ability to strike fear into the heart of the enemy.

struggle and try to get away to get back to its mother, crying and bleating and protesting. But to no avail. The rope around its leg was too strong and the post was driven too deep. Eventually, the baby elephant would give up struggling.

Each day, the owner would take the baby elephant away and tie it to a post for several hours. In almost no time at all, the baby elephant would accept that, when it was tied to a post, it was helpless. The baby elephant developed the greatest malaise of the modern world, what psychologists call learned helplessness.

The Elephant Gives Up

When the elephant grew up into a five-ton beast, the largest land animal in the world, all the owner had to do was tie a rope the size of a dog leash around the elephant's leg and it would immediately become passive and stop moving or struggling. The owner could then tie the other end of this rope to a tent post driven a few inches into the ground. The elephant, capable of breaking through fences and knocking down houses, would simply stand and wait quietly until the owner came back to take him to work.

As children, the same thing happens to us. At an early age, our parents begin to say to us words like "No!" or "Stop that," or "Get away from there!" or "Don't touch that!" Sometimes the parent would back up these words with spanks

The owner could then tie the other end of this leash to a tent post driven a few inches into the ground.

or other kinds of physical punishment. The growing child would soon start to feel small, incompetent, incapable, weak, and afraid to try anything new or different.

THE ROOT OF HELPLESSNESS

Most people have had these childhood experiences. Just like the elephant, when you grow up whenever you are confronted with something new, different, unexpected, or unsure your natural reaction is the same, "I can't! I can't! I can't!"

This fear of failure then holds you back from trying new things, taking risks, moving out of your comfort zone, and thinking outside the box. Instead of thinking of all the ways you could benefit and grow from trying or doing something different, you only think of the possible downside and the negative things that might happen.

Like the Indian elephant, you become passive. This is the state of mind of fully 80 percent of the population.

SET BIG GOALS

Here's a question for you: Would you like to be happy, healthy, popular, thin, and rich?

> Like the Indian elephant, you become passive.

Most people say, "What a dumb question! Of course I would like to be happy, healthy, popular, thin, and rich."

You think you do, but in your heart of hearts you probably don't believe that it's possible for you. How can you tell? By looking at what you are doing. If you sincerely want to achieve these great goals, you would be out there working on them all day every day and nothing could stop you from achieving them.

YOUR ACTIONS TELL THE TRUTH

It is not what you say, wish, hope, or intend that matters, it is only what you do. Your actions on an hour by hour, minute by minute basis tell you and everyone around you who you really are and what you really want.

Good habits are hard to form but easy to live with.

You are what you are and where you are today because of all of your previous choices up until now. You cannot change the past, but you can change the future. You can accomplish more and different things in the future by making better choices in the present.

THE KEY TO SUCCESS

Since 95 percent of what you do, positive or negative, is determined by your habits, the secret to creating a wonderful future for yourself is to develop new habits that are consistent with the person you want to be and the things you want to accomplish.

The truth is that bad habits are easy to form but hard to live with. Good habits are hard to form but easy to live with.

The wonderful discovery is that once you develop a new, positive, life-enhancing habit, it soon becomes automatic and easy. It even becomes harder to revert to a negative habit than to practice a better one because of the feelings of happiness and personal satisfaction that the new habit gives you.

NEW HABIT PATTERN DEVELOPMENT

How do you develop a new, positive habit? The same way that you developed an old negative habit. Through practice and repetition. Here is the formula:

1. **Develop one habit at a time.** Start with something simple, a success habit of top people, like punctuality.

2. **Make a decision that you are going to be punctual from now on.** Decisiveness is extremely powerful in new habit pattern development. The reason that most people are performing at a low level is because they never decided to perform at a higher one.

3. **Create a positive affirmation that is phrased as if you already had your new habit.** Say something like, "I am punctual for every meeting and appointment."

Repeat this over and over, like a mantra, until it is accepted by your subconscious mind as a command. Once your subconscious mind accepts these new instructions, you find yourself becoming more punctual and actually enjoying the experience.

Vince Lombardi, the football coach, was famous for what they called "Lombardi time." Lombardi time was defined as "fifteen minutes before the scheduled time." If the bus was scheduled to leave at 9:00 a.m., all the players were trained to be there at 8:45 a.m. If you weren't there, the bus would leave without you.

Start practicing Lombardi time in every area of your life. Make a decision not just to be on time but to be ten to fifteen minutes early for every appointment.

4. **Visualize yourself as if you already had the habit of punctuality.** Create a clear mental picture of yourself behaving exactly as you would like to in the future. Remember, all improvements in personal performance begin with an improvement in your mental pictures.

5. **Act as if you already had the habit that you desire.** Ask, "How would I behave if I was one of the most punctual people around?" Behave the way you think other punctual people behave. Pretend that you are already the person you intend to be.

6. **Create the feelings of pride, happiness, and self-control that you would have when you are always punctual.** These emotions of pride, self-confidence,

and self-respect drive the habit and behavior deeper into your subconscious mind, making your new habit automatic, faster, and easier.

Here is a great discovery: **the development and practice of any positive habit strengthens and reinforces all your other positive habits at the same time. Any weakness or letting yourself off the hook on a particular discipline will weaken all your other positive habits as well.**

THE WORST DISEASE

The worst disease, the one that undermines and sabotages most of success, is called "excusitis." This is defined as "an inflammation of the excuse-making gland." It is invariably fatal to success.

One of the hallmarks of "fully functioning people," is that they "never complain, never explain." They never make excuses or justify their behavior. They either do it or they don't do it, but they never whine about "getting stuck in traffic" or one of the numerous excuses that weak people use to justify being late.

▶ ▶ ▶

The worst disease, the one that undermines and sabotages most of succcess, is called "excusitis."

Eliminate failure language from your vocabulary. Refuse to say things like "I'll try," or "I'll do my best."

These expressions are excuses for failure in advance. When someone says, "I'll try to do it by that time," what they are saying is that "I'm giving you a clear signal that I'm going to fail. I'm not going to do it on time. You can't blame me if it doesn't get done."

Making excuses makes you feel small and insecure. And they don't fool anyone. Everyone knows that the excuse-makers are the incompetent and undependable people in any situation.

FANTASY ISLAND

We joke and say that everyone wants to be successful, wealthy, thin, popular, and enjoy a wonderful life. But before they get started they decide that they need a little vacation. So they all go to a wonderful mental vacation place, an island called "Someday I'll."

They say, "Someday I'll work harder and get promoted."

"Someday I'll read that book and upgrade my skills."

An island called "Someday I'll."

"Someday I'll start that weight loss program and get rid of these extra pounds."

"Someday I'll learn how to manage my time so that I can be more productive." Et cetera, et cetera, et cetera.

And who are they surrounded with on Someday I'll? They are surrounded by other people who are also on Someday I'll. And what is the most common subject of conversation on Someday I'll? It is "favorite excuses."

Favorite Excuses

People who take up residence on this particular isle like to trade excuses. "What's your reason for being here on the island?" they ask each other. And then they go back and forth sharing their favorite reasons for failing to live up to their potentials.

As Mark Twain said, "There are a thousand excuses for failure but never a good reason."

So here is the secret of success: Vote yourself off the island!

No more "excusitis" for you. No more trips to Someday I'll. Instead, one by one, resolve to develop the habits of high performance. Start this very minute. Select one habit that you would like

to develop and go to work on it for a solid month. Practice every day. Never allow an exception. If you do slip, as you will from time to time, immediately get back to practicing your new habit.

Do this over and over until it finally becomes easy and automatic. Then move on to the next habit that you need to develop to become all you can become. More importantly, develop the habit of getting started and keeping going on your most important task.

"Stay focused, go after your dreams and keep moving toward your goals."—LL Cool J

CHAPTER TWO

TAKE
CHARGE
of Your Life

> "Hold yourself responsible for a higher standard than anybody else expects of you. Never excuse yourself."
> —*Henry Ward Beecher*

Your goal is to feel powerful, purposeful, competent, and capable of doing anything you need to achieve any goal you can set for yourself. But, before you do anything you have to do something else first.

You have to accept 100 percent responsibility for the person you are today, for everything you have ever done or accomplished, and for everything that you achieve in the months and years ahead.

You are responsible. No one is coming to the rescue. It is all up to you.

THE BIG DIFFERENCE

The acceptance of personal responsibility is the great divider between winners and losers, between leaders and followers, between rich people and poor people.

When we are young we become accustomed to our parents making all the important decisions for us. They decide what we will wear, what we will eat, what we will do, and where we will go. This is the way it should be when you are a child.

Ideally, as you grow older you take on more and more responsibility for your life until, when you become an adult, you take on 100 percent responsibility. You are on your own. You make your own choices and decisions. You do what you want. You refuse to do what you don't want to do. You are in charge.

ESCAPE FROM DEPENDENCY

But most people, deep down inside, have the "dependency habit" in one or more areas of their lives. They think, feel, hope, and wish that sometime, somehow, someone will come along and save them. Someone will teach and train them, giving them a job to do and a place to work, while making all the important decisions in their work lives.

Most people, deep down inside, have the "dependency habit" in one or more areas of their lives.

They transfer their sense of dependency from their parents to their bosses and companies, becoming passive, like the Indian elephant, and they wait for someone to come along and tell them what to do.

TIME SLIPS BY

They take the first job that someone offers them, put their heads down, and say, "If you want to get along, you have to go along."

Then, one day they lift up their heads, look around, and find that they are sixty-five years old. They have finished their useful work life, their bank accounts are almost empty, and they are looking forward to many years of surviving on limited savings, pensions, and Social Security.

This story from writer Joseph Campbell illustrates this point. Campbell writes about going out for dinner at a small neighborhood restaurant. At the next table a husband and wife were sitting with their ten-year-old son. Referring to the food that had been served to him, the son said, "I don't like it." The boy's father quite sternly told the son, "That is your dinner, you will eat it."

The little boy replied, "I don't want to!"

At this, the father became angry and blew up. He said loudly, "You don't want to? You don't want to? I never did anything I wanted to in my whole life!"

THE ROOT OF UNHAPPINESS

When I began studying success I stumbled across a body of teaching that changed my life forever. It said that the primary aim in life is positive emotions—to be happy. The only obstacle to happiness and positive emotion is negative emotion. Therefore, the entire business of life is the elimination of negative emotions of all kinds.

Wow! Could it be that simple? But as I studied the subject of success and happiness, I realized that the greatest enemies of mankind, of you, me, and of everyone else, are negative emotions—of all kinds.

If we can just get rid of our negative emotions, our minds should automatically fill with positive emotions, emotions of peace, joy, and happiness.

THE BIGGEST PROBLEM

There are more than fifty negative emotions that have been identified, and there are libraries full of books on their root causes. Psychologists, psychoanalysts, and psychotherapists help people deal with those feelings that make them unhappy and interfere with the quality of their lives, as do coaches, counselors, ministers, therapists, and good friends.

But, after thousands of hours of research, I finally found the secret—the way to get rid of negative emotions, once and for all, and almost immediately.

What I discovered was that although there are many negative emotions—envy, resentment, fear, doubt, jealousy, hatred, anger, and hypersensitivity to the thoughts, words, and opinions of others—they all come down to one root cause: **blame.**

The Root Cause of Negativity

It is not possible for you to hold a negative emotion of any kind without blaming someone or something for your unhappiness. You blame your parents, your siblings, your romantic relationships, your bad bosses, and the people that lied to you, cheated you, hurt you, or took advantage of you in some way.

You blame wealthy people for the fact that there are poor people. You blame successful people for the fact that there are failures. You blame the members of the opposite political party for all the problems in life and in the world.

Mostly, you blame other people for something they have done or not done that has hurt you in some way.

▶ ▶ ▶

Mostly, you blame other people for something they have done or not done that has hurt you in some way.

Stop Blaming Others

How do you stop blaming? This is

the breakthrough discovery. It is both simple and effective. It works 100 percent of the time. It transforms your mind from negative to positive, sometimes in a few seconds. Here it is: say the words, "I am responsible!" whenever you feel angry or upset about anyone or anything.

The words "I am responsible" are great neutralizers. Just like when you pull the lamp cord out of the socket the lamp goes out, when you say "I am responsible," your negative emotions switch off and go out instantly.

You cannot say, "I am responsible" and be angry, worried, or scared at the same time. The words "I am responsible" put you back in the driver's seat. They enable you to take complete charge of your life, turning you from a victim into a victor. They take you from feeling weak and insecure to feeling strong and self-reliant. The words "I am responsible" repeated over and over and over again reprogram your mind and turn you into a completely positive, powerful, and forceful person.

The words "I am responsible" put you back in the driver's seat.

SUCCESS VERSUS FAILURE

Each person has a "success mechanism" as well as a "failure mechanism" in his or her brain. As it happens, your failure mechanism is your "default setting." It goes off automatically, continually activating your tendency to think negative thoughts.

When you are sitting by yourself, driving, watching television, or in any work or personal situation, you can automatically find yourself thinking about the things that make you angry or unhappy.

You talk about them with your friends and family. You bring them up at the family dinner table. They keep you awake at night. You construct imaginary conversations about them, even with people who are not present, and sometimes you argue with them angrily. Everyone does this occasionally.

TRIGGER YOUR SUCCESS MECHANISM

Your success mechanism, however, is triggered by a goal, by your accepting complete responsibility for your life and then getting busy working on something that you care about, something that you really want. (We'll talk about this more in Chapter Four).

Here is the kicker: instead of using your brilliant mind to think about all the justifications and reasons you have to feel negatively toward someone who you feel caused your situation, you should use that incredible mind of yours to think of all the reasons why you might be responsible for

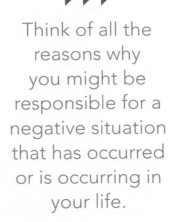

▶ ▶ ▶
Think of all the reasons why you might be responsible for a negative situation that has occurred or is occurring in your life.

a negative situation that has occurred or is occurring in your life.

When I coach and counsel people sometimes they will talk about their failed marriage, how terrible their spouse was, and how angry they still feel about what he or she did or didn't do to them.

YOU WERE RESPONSIBLE

Then I remind them that they were responsible. It was they who decided to marry that person, even if they had misgivings, which they probably had. It was they who decided to stay in the marriage. It was they who put up with and accepted the negative things that the other person did or said. They were and **are** still responsible.

The rule for happiness is to never be upset or angry about something that you cannot change.

At the very least, you are responsible for what you do from this point forward. The rule for happiness is to never be upset or angry about something that you cannot change. And you cannot change a past event. All you can do with an unhappy experience is learn from it, and then let it go. Accept 100 percent responsibility.

THINK ABOUT WHY

Even better, think through the negative situation that still upsets you and think of all the ways in which you actually were responsible for what happened. Instead of mulling continually over what the other person did or didn't do, think about all the things that you did or didn't do to get yourself into that situation in the first place.

As you accept responsibility and think of all the reasons why you were responsible, your negativity disappears. In almost no time something that has been making you angry for months or even years dissipates, like cigarette smoke in a large room, and is gone forever.

KEEP EMOTIONAL CONTROL

Eleanor Roosevelt said, "No one can make you feel inferior without your consent."

When you blame someone else for something that they did or didn't do, you are allowing them to control your emotions—at long distance. You are actually allowing them to make you feel small, inferior, and angry. Is this what you had in mind?

Follow the advice of Walt Whitman who said, "Keep your face always toward the sunshine—and shadows will fall behind you."

When you accept responsibility you take full charge of your life. **You move from childhood to adulthood in one bold stride. You become a master of** circumstances rather than a victim of circumstances. All your negativity dissipates and all that is left are positive emotions that enrich and enhance your life.

MAKE A DECISION

Decide today to accept 100 percent responsibility for everything you are or ever will be. It can be the biggest and most exhilarating decision you ever make. Making this decision sets you free to get started and keep going toward what you really want. No more excuses.

"Being best is a false goal, you have to measure success on your own terms."—Damien Hirst

CHAPTER THREE

Dare to Go
FORWARD

> "Nothing splendid has ever been achieved except by those who dared believe that something inside of them was superior to circumstance."
>
> —*Bruce Barton*

One of the most important requirements for success is action-orientation. This is the internal motivation to get going immediately on a goal or project. Action orientation is expressed in a sense of urgency and an impatience to get the job done quickly. It is one of the most important qualities of the most successful people in any field.

The biggest obstacle to taking action immediately is fear—fear of failure, loss, embarrassment, criticism, or ridicule. To achieve all that is possible for you, you

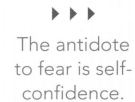

The antidote to fear is self-confidence.

must consciously and deliberately take control of the fears that hold you back.

SELF-CONFIDENCE CANCELS FEAR

The antidote to fear is self-confidence. Self-confidence gives you the energy, enthusiasm, and drive to overcome any obstacle, internal or external, in the pursuit of your goal.

Self-confidence is based on a foundation of courage, and courage is the key quality that leads to success.

As Winston Churchill said, "Courage is rightly considered the foremost of the virtues, for upon it, all others depend."

Margaret Thatcher said it this way, "Everything comes down to courage at the sticking point."

Just imagine! **How would your life be different if you were absolutely fearless? How would your life be different if you had so much self-confidence in your ability to succeed that you would take any risk, and dare to go forward under any circumstances?**

Everyone Is Afraid

As it happens, everyone is afraid of some things, and often, many things. The only difference is how you deal with the normal and natural fears that you experience each day.

Ralph Waldo Emerson gave us the solution: "Do the thing you fear, and the death of fear is certain."

The way you overcome your fears and develop unshakable levels of courage and self-confidence is to deliberately do the very thing that you fear, over and over, until the fear is gone.

▶ ▶ ▶

Ralph Waldo Emerson gave us the solution: "Do the thing you fear, and the death of fear is certain."

One of the greatest fears that holds us back is the fear of rejection. This usually comes from destructive criticism in early childhood. As adults we still may be hypersensitive to the opinions, real or imagined, of others. This concern over what other people may think about us often holds us back from trying in the first place.

A VALUABLE SUCCESS PRINCIPLE

Never do or don't do anything because you are afraid of what people may think about you. Because the fact is, no one is thinking about you at all.

It is amazing how many people stay in a bad job, unhappy relationship, bad marriage, or a difficult situation of any kind because they are so concerned that people will be critical of them if they decide to get out of the situation and walk away. When they finally do muster up the courage to walk away, they are often surprised that no one really cares. Nobody is thinking about them at all.

FACE THE FEAR

In *Hamlet*, Shakespeare says, ". . . take arms against a sea of troubles, and, by opposing, end them." The interesting discovery is that as you move toward the person or situation that you fear and take action in spite of your fear, your fear goes away and is replaced by courage.

However, if you back away from the fear-inducing person or situation the fear continues to grow, and soon consumes your thoughts and feelings, distracting you during the day and keeping you awake at night.

A young journalist, Arthur Gordon, was interviewing Thomas

If you back away from the fear-inducing person or situation, the fear continues to grow.

J. Watson Sr., the founder of IBM, and asked him, "Mr. Watson, how can I be more successful faster?"

Watson replied with these classic words, "If you want to increase your success rate, double your failure rate… That's where you'll find success—on the far side of failure."

Learn to Be Unafraid

When I interview wealthy people, I am always surprised to learn that many of them, perhaps the majority, started off their careers as salespeople cold-calling to sell their products and services. By facing their fears of failure and rejection over and over, they eventually reached the point where they weren't afraid of failing.

The very idea of cold-calling is scary, even traumatic, for many people. I have spoken to countless people who took sales jobs that required cold-calling and literally collapsed in fear within a few hours and went back to working for wages.

The only way you overcome your fear of cold-calling, or anything else, is to do it over and over again. In my sales seminars, I teach the "100 Call Method." I tell my sales professionals that the fastest way to blast yourself out of a sales slump and to double your sales income is for you to go out and make one hundred calls as fast as you possibly can, and don't care about the outcome.

FORGET ABOUT REJECTION

Imagine that someone offered to pay you ten, twenty, or thirty dollars for the next one hundred people that you contacted either by phone or in person, and you would get paid whether or not that

person liked you, hated you, bought from you, or even slammed down the phone. What would you do?

The answer is that if you had no fear of rejection, you would call your one hundred people as fast as you possibly could. And when you do the most amazing thing happens. By calling people, without caring whether they buy or not, you will develop more energy and confidence than ever before. And many of the people in your one hundred calls will turn out to be your best customers in the weeks and months ahead.

MAKE IT A GAME

In the book, *The Happiness of Pursuit*, the author tells story after story about people who decided to overcome their fears and embark on journeys and adventures that they might have thought about for years but never had the courage to pursue.

In one story, a young, extremely shy man in Houston, Texas, who was plagued by a fear of rejection and criticism, decided to go out and ask one hundred people if he could do something that he had never done before.

▶ ▶ ▶

He resolved to go out and make one hundred outrageous requests.

He asked people on the street if he could hug them, a fire chief if he could slide down the pole in the fire hall, and others if they would give him things for free. He resolved to go out and make one hundred outrageous requests, not caring whether or not people said "no." At the end of his experiment, most of his shyness, sensitivity, and fear of rejection were gone forever.

DO WHAT SCARES YOU

Darren Hardy, the publisher of *Success* magazine said, "To be scared is to give up your power. Do what scares you and you gain it back."

He tells the story of wanting to buy a bicycle as a twelve-year-old but having no money. The thing that scared him the most was asking people to buy something and being rejected. So he got a job with a direct sales company selling a small product to passersby on the sidewalk.

He mustered up his courage and stood there all day long approaching strangers, offering his product, and asking them to buy. Most of them rejected him outright. But by the end of two days of work, during which he made sales and earned money, he was completely unafraid of cold-calling and prospecting for the rest of his life. By the time he was twenty-five he was a millionaire.

LEARNING EXPERIENCES

In a Harvard study, they found that leaders seldom use the word "failure." Instead they use the term "learning experiences."

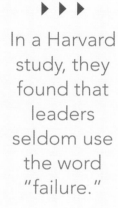

▶ ▶ ▶

In a Harvard study, they found that leaders seldom use the word "failure."

They say, "This was a valuable learning experience," or, "This was an expensive learning experience." Or often they will say, "This was a painful learning experience." But they never used the word failure.

In business today, to be successful you must be prepared to have an enormous number of "learning experiences" to find the right product or service combination and to do the necessary things to sell effectively in an increasingly competitive market.

FOUR STEPS TO SUCCESS

The process to succeed in business today is simple. It has four parts: (1) decide what you want to do, (2) take action immediately, (3) fail and learn quickly, (4) try it again, over and over, until you succeed.

NO FAILURE, ONLY FEEDBACK

The fact is that there is no such thing as failure, only feedback. You learn to succeed by failing, so you should not fear it. In fact, you should look forward to every failure experience, knowing that each one is moving you closer to the success you desire.

Journalist Dorothea Brande wrote, "Act as if it were impossible to fail, and it shall be."

Mark Victor Hansen echoed this thought when he said, "Whatever you want, wants you."

From now on, whatever you want, go for it! **Take a chance. Move out of your comfort zone. Try, try again, and then try once more.**

PICK UP THE PACE

The faster you fail, the faster you will succeed. And even better, the more often you fail, the more courage and confidence you will develop until you finally become unstoppable. Nothing will stop you from getting started and keeping on.

CHAPTER FOUR

DECIDE
What You Really Want

> "Within you right now is the power to do things you never dreamed possible. This power becomes available to you just as soon as you can change your beliefs."
> —*Maxwell Maltz*

Perhaps the greatest discovery in all of human history is this: you become what you think about—most of the time.

This is the foundation principle of all religions, philosophy, psychology, and success. As Ralph Waldo Emerson said, "A man is what he thinks about all day long."

In the Bible, it says, "As a man thinketh in his heart, so is he."

Your outer world tends to be a mirror image of your inner world. If you want to change something in your outer world, you have to go to work on the one thing in the entire world that you can control—your thoughts.

YOU HAVE TO BE HUNGRY

Successful people in every field have been interviewed many times to learn what enables them to accomplish exceedingly more than the average person. Perhaps the most important quality of successful people is ambition. They are hungry. They have a burning desire to accomplish more than they've ever accomplished before.

This intense desire for success and achievement is what motivates them, energizes, and drives them to overcome any obstacle and to persist until they achieve their goals.

What is it that you want more than anything else? What gets you out of bed in the morning and drives you to work hard all day long?

YOU NEED A BIG GOAL

What is your **BHAG** (Big Hairy Audacious Goal)? What is the one goal that, if you accomplished it, could make the greatest possible difference in your life?

What is the one goal that, if you accomplished it, would make the greatest possible difference in your life?

Napoleon Hill wrote in *Think and Grow Rich*, "People only begin to become great when they decide upon their major definite purpose in life." What is yours?

In my seminars I have found that most people have no idea about their most important goal. I would then tell them, "Then your major definite purpose in life must be to discover your major definite purpose in life."

The good news is that when you have big, exciting, important goals you will be continuously motivated to take action to achieve them. Nothing will hold you back.

GOALS ARE CLEAR AND SPECIFIC

One of the worst mistakes a person can make, which is invariably fatal to success, is to think that they already have goals when all they really have are wishes.

When I ask a room full of seminar attendees, "How many people here have goals?" Every hand goes up. Then I ask people in

the audience at random, "What are your goals?"

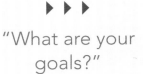

▶ ▶ ▶

"What are your goals?"

They say things like: "I want to be successful." "I want to make a lot of money." "I want to be happy." "I want to have a happy family." "I want to travel." "I want to be a millionaire." And so on. But these are not goals; these are fantasies, wishes, hopes, dreams, and illusions. Everybody has them. These are aspirations that are common to mankind and always have been. But they are not goals.

CHANGE YOUR LIFE

All over the world people come up to me and say pretty much the same words, "You changed my life; you made me rich." I have heard these words hundreds of thousands of times. When I ask them, "What was it in my books or courses that helped you so much?" They always smile broadly and say, "It was the goals."

It's always the goals. The major turning point in my own life was the same. It happened when I was twenty-four. I discovered goals for the first time. Within a month after writing down a series of goals on a scrap of paper my whole life had changed.

As a result of a remarkable series of events, occurrences, and coincidences, I had achieved almost all the goals I had written down one month before. It was like touching a hot electric wire and getting a shock. I was never the same again.

When you have big goals that you really want to achieve, nothing will stop you from taking action and doing whatever you need to do to achieve those goals.

PERSONAL STRATEGIC PLANNING

When I work with corporations we go through a basic process of corporate goal setting that you can apply to yourself. It has seven parts:

1. **Your values.** What do you believe in? What is important to you? Of all the things that you believe in and care about, what is more important than anything else? Values clarification is the starting point of high performance, for an individual or for an organization.

2. **Your vision.** Imagine you could wave a magic wand and project yourself forward five years, and your life would be perfect in every way. What would it look like? What would you be doing? How much money

would you be earning? And how would your perfect life, sometime in the future, be different from today?

When you develop an exciting vision for your future life, for your business, your career, your family, your health, and your financial situation, your whole life begins to change. Your inner world vision starts to become your outer world of experience.

3. **Your mission.** What do you want to achieve with your life? If you are in business, what do you want to achieve for your customers? What do you want to achieve for other people, your family, and the customers you want to serve?

A person with a clear mission for his or her future is much more determined and energetic than a person who is just going through the motions at work and then going home and watching television.

4. **Your purpose.** Why do you do what you do rather than something else? Why have you selected this particular career or business? What is it about your chosen field that excites you, inspires you, and motivates you every single day? Friedrich Nietzsche, the philosopher, said, "He who has a why to live can bear almost any how." What is your "why?"

5. **Your goals.** These are the ultimate results that you want to achieve. This is where you align your values, vision, mission, and purpose and focus them on a single point.

6. **Your priorities.** What are the most important actions that you can take each day to achieve your most important goals, consistent with your values, vision, mission, and purpose?

7. **Your actions.** What are you going to do immediately, now, this minute, to achieve what is most important to you?

It turns out that the big difference in income inequality is not between the 99 percent versus the 1 percent. It is actually between the 3 percent who have clear, specific, written goals and plans, and the other 97 percent who do not.

SETTING YOUR GOALS

If you are sincere about joining the top 3 percent, here are some tips that you can use for the rest of your life to achieve your goals. They will enable you to accomplish anything that you really want, if you want it badly enough.

1. **Decide exactly what you want.** Be specific. Your goal should be so clear that a six-year-old child could understand it and explain it to another six-year-old child and tell you how close you are to achieving it.

2. **Write it down.** Only 3 percent of adults have written goals and they earn on average, *ten times* as much as other people with the same talents, education, ability, and opportunities.

3. **Set a deadline.** A goal has been called a "dream with a deadline."

Set subdeadlines if your goal is big enough. A deadline acts as a "forcing system" for your subconscious mind. It gets you out of bed in the morning and drives you all day long to achieve your goals on schedule.

If you don't achieve a particular goal by a specific deadline, simply set a new deadline. Remember, there are no unrealistic goals; only unrealistic deadlines.

4. **Make a list.** Write down everything that you can think of that you can do to achieve your goal. As Henry Ford said, "Nothing is particularly hard if you divide it into small jobs."

5. **Organize the list.** Create a checklist and write down everything that you will have to do in sequence, by time. What will you have to do first, second, third, and so on?

The rule is that every minute spent in planning will save you ten minutes in execution. Once you have a checklist, you work from it every single day. If you have never done this before, you will be astonished at how much you get accomplished and how fast you accomplish it.

6. **Take action.** Do something immediately on your major goal. Don't

▶ ▶ ▶

Take the first step.

procrastinate and don't hesitate. Take the first step.

7. **Do something every day.** From this moment onward, do something every day, seven days a week, that moves you toward your most important goal. Never miss a day.

By doing something on your goal every day, you begin to develop momentum, which causes you to move forward faster and easier. As a result, you find it natural to get going and keep going every day.

THE TEN-GOAL METHOD

Take a clean sheet of paper and write the word "Goals" at the top of the page along with today's date.

By doing something on your goal every day, you begin to develop momentum.

Then, write down ten goals that you'd like to achieve in the next twelve months.

These can be one-week goals, one-month goals, six-month goals and so on, but they should be achievable within the coming twelve months. It seems that goals that are achievable in less than a year have far more motivational power than longer-term goals, which you can set later.

THE KEY QUESTION

Once you have written down ten goals, ask yourself this question: "Which one goal on this list, if I were to achieve it within twenty-four hours, would have the greatest positive impact on my life?"

Whatever your answer, that goal then becomes your major definite purpose, your "BHAG." This becomes the organizing principle of your life—your focal point, your point of concentration.

From now on, work on this goal every day. When you get up in the morning, think about your goal. As you go through your day, think about the goal. In the evening, review your progress toward your goal.

▶ ▶ ▶

When you get up in the morning, think about your goal.

CREATE YOUR OWN MIRACLE

Something miraculous happens when you begin to focus single-mindedly on your most important goal. You start to make progress on all your other goals simultaneously. Your whole life begins to move forward, like an army on the march.

You will often achieve more in the next few months than many people achieve in several years. But it starts with one big goal. This is your greatest single responsibility to yourself and your future. Get started on it and keep going every day.

" **Our goals** can only be reached through a vehicle of a plan, in which we must fervently believe, and upon which we must vigorously act. There is no other route to success."

—Pablo Picasso

CHAPTER FIVE

OVERCOME
Procrastination

> "He who every morning plans the transactions of the day and follows out that plan, carries a thread that will guide him through the labyrinth of the most busy life."
> —*Victor Hugo*

All success comes from task completion, from getting started on a job and then completing it as soon as possible.

Like all other habits, procrastination is also a learned behavior. It starts off in early childhood and grows over the years. The habit of procrastination among adults is perhaps the number one reason for underachievement and failure in every area.

Abraham Lincoln said, "Things may come to those who wait, but only the things left by those who hustle." In overcoming procrastination, you need to go to the extreme of immediate action, over and over, almost as a lifestyle, until procrastination is replaced with speedy task completion.

Abraham Lincoln said, "Things may come to those who wait, but only the things left by those who hustle."

EVERYONE PROCRASTINATES

As it happens, everyone procrastinates, just on different things. Top time managers procrastinate just as well as poor time managers.

But the most productive people procrastinate on those things of the lowest value, on the bottom 80 percent of tasks that represent only 20 percent or less of results.

Average people on the other hand, procrastinate on the 20 percent of activities that represent 80 percent of the value of everything they do.

From now on, practice "creative procrastination." Consciously decide that you will not do low value activities, until you have completed your higher value tasks.

WHAT HOLDS YOU BACK?

To overcome procrastination, you must identify the factors that are causing you to procrastinate today, and think about how many of them actually apply to you.

1. **Lack of clarity.** If you are unclear or unsure about the most important thing to do, you will often end up doing things of low value, or nothing at all. Fully 95 percent of success in life comes from becoming absolutely clear about your top goals and the most important things that you can do, every minute, to achieve them.

2. **Lack of ambition.** How badly do you want it? If you do not have an intense, burning desire, or a big enough reason for starting and completing a task, you often never get started at all. You develop the disease of "excusitis," and continually assure yourself and others that you are going to get started on that big task soon.

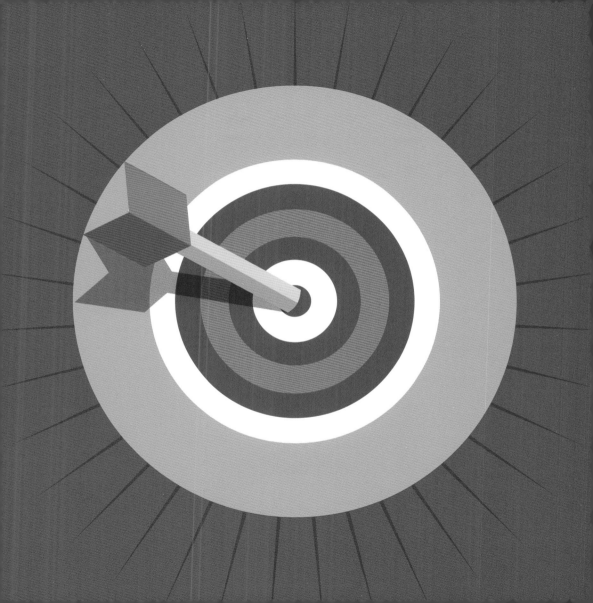

3. **Lack of priorities.** Because you have not planned out your task, and organized it by sequence and priority, you are often unsure of what to do first. As a result, you do nothing at all.

4. **Overload.** Often, you have too many tasks or activities to do for the limited amount of time that you have available. As a result, you just throw up your hands and tell yourself that you'll "do it tomorrow."

5. **Lack of preparation.** You don't have everything you need at hand to start and complete the job. Very often, the act of bringing together all the materials you require actually helps launch you into the task.

6. **Lack of energy.** You need eight to nine hours of sleep per night, combined with healthy, nutritious foods,

to be fully energized to do your best work. As Vince Lombardi said, "Fatigue make cowards of us all."

When you are physically tired or mentally burned out you lack the energy necessary to start and complete important tasks.

7. **Lack of knowledge.** If you have not learned everything you need to know about your job, and you do not know what to do or how to do it, it is quite common to procrastinate until you get more information.

8. **Lack of self-discipline.** This is probably the worst weakness of all. You lack the willpower to get yourself going and to keep yourself moving.

How many of these factors apply to you? **They probably apply to every person at one time or another. To reach the top of your field, you must see these factors as enemies, as obstacles that are blocking you from fulfilling your true potential.**

BECOMING ACTION-ORIENTED

There are several "tricks" you can play on yourself to overcome procrastination and launch yourself into your most important task.

1. **Make a checklist.** You have heard that "failure to plan is planning to fail."

Make an orderly checklist of each task in a larger job, with a sequence from the first task to the last task. The very act of having a track to run on dramatically reduces your tendency to procrastinate.

2. **Salami slice the task.** You would never think of eating a loaf of salami all at once. Instead, you eat it a slice at a time. Do the same thing with each large task. Slice off a small piece of the task and complete that one activity. You don't have to do everything. Just do one small thing. That will often be enough to get you going.

3. **Swiss cheese technique.** Punch a hole, like a hole in Swiss cheese, in your task and resolve to work for five or ten straight minutes before stopping and doing

something else. When you look at your task, pick one small part and say emphatically "I will do this now!"

4. **Use the 20/80 rule.** Twenty percent of the things you do account for 80 percent of your results. Identify the 20 percent of tasks that will account for 80 percent of your success in this project. Sometimes, the first 20 percent of tasks that you do, like planning and organizing, will account for 80 percent of the entire task.

Twenty percent of the things you do acount for 80 percent of your results.

5. **Reward yourself.** Set up a schedule of rewards for starting, working on, and completing a particular

job. Reward yourself with a cup of coffee for doing one thing on your list. Reward yourself with a stretch break for making ten customer calls. Reward yourself with a dinner out for hitting a numerical or financial goal.

6. **Promise others.** Tell other people that you are going to complete a specific task by a specific time. When you know others are watching you and you have committed to doing a particular job on time, you will be much more motivated to get started, push through, and complete the job.

7. **Begin immediately.** Start work on a major task first thing each morning before checking your email, cell phone, or messages.

8. **Focus on each task.** Select your most important task and start on it first thing, and then work until that task is 100 percent complete. This is called single-handling, one of the most powerful time management techniques ever developed.

YOU FEEL LIKE A WINNER

When you complete a task, even a small task, you experience a rush of endorphins. You feel happy and motivated. You feel stimulated into starting on your next task so that you can once again enjoy that happy feeling of accomplishment.

When you complete a task, even a small task, you experience a rush of endorphins.

In the final analysis, the very best reputation you can develop is one for speed and dependability. When people are completely confident that they can give you a job, walk away, and not have to think about it again because of your reputation for task completion, you will become a magnet for bigger, better, and more important tasks. When people know that, whatever the goal, you will get started on it and keep going until it is complete, your future will be guaranteed.

CHAPTER SIX

Become a Lifelong
LEARNER

> "Live as if you were going to die tomorrow. Learn as if you were going to live forever."
> —Mahatma Gandhi

The main obstacles to success are doubt and fear, of all kinds. First, you doubt your ability to succeed greatly, to do your job well, and to perform better than other people. Self-doubt is one of the most destructive of all negative emotions. It can cause you to quit before you even get started.

Second, you fear that you may not succeed. This obstacle, fear of failure, which we have talked about before, paralyzes you both consciously and unconsciously and holds you back, tripping you up every step of the way.

THE BEST ANTIDOTES

The antidotes to doubt and fear are knowledge and skill. The more knowledge you have on any subject the less doubt you have about your ability to succeed. When you become an expert in a subject you develop such high levels of self-confidence that you are soon willing to take on bigger and bigger challenges, and accomplish more and more in that area.

The antidote to fear is skill. When you have taken the time to plan, prepare, and practice over and over, you eventually come to know, deep inside, that you can do this particular job and eventually anything you put your mind to.

BECOME A LIFELONG LEARNER

There are certain thinking styles that divide top people from average people. One of them is the difference between "informed thinking" and "uninformed thinking." Many of the biggest mistakes that people make come from acting without having gathered enough information. As a result, they often lack essential facts that cause them to make mistakes, fail, and fall flat on their faces.

But the better informed you are in any area, the more confidence you have that you can make the right decision and achieve the results that you desire.

SELF-MADE BILLIONAIRES

In *Forbes* magazine's 2015 edition on billionaires, they found that 66 percent of them were self-made. They had started with little or nothing and earned more than one billion dollars in a lifetime.

Many of them are younger than forty and some of them are younger than thirty.

When they asked these billionaires why they felt they had been so successful, many of them attributed their success at least partially to continuous learning. They were like sponges. They were constantly absorbing new information from every source. They had discovered that one idea or insight that you pick up from continuous learning can be all you need to start a fortune.

NO SUCH THING AS LUCK

Many of these wealthy people say, "I was just lucky." However, when you study their backgrounds, and the many things that they did and tried in the years before they became successful, you will find that it was not luck at all. Instead, it was a matter of probabilities.

The law of probability says that there is a probability that anything can happen. By using probability equations, the likelihood of almost anything happening can be calculated with tremendous accuracy.

In its simplest terms, if you throw enough darts at a dartboard, even if you start off largely unskilled, you will eventually hit a bull's-eye. This is not a matter of luck; it's a matter of probability.

BECOME A MILLIONAIRE

According to Spectrum's *Market Insights*, in 2015 there are more than ten million millionaires in the United States alone. There is a probability that you too can become a millionaire or a multi-millionaire. Your job is to increase the probabilities in your favor by doing more and more of the things that make it more likely that you will pass that million-dollar mark.

One of the things that you can do to increase the probabilities of financial success is to "cast a wide net." Keep upgrading your knowledge and skills and gathering more information as if your future depended on it, because it does.

▶ ▶ ▶

Keep upgrading your knowledge and skills and gathering more information as if your future depended on it, because it does.

It is said that Warren Buffet reads and studies 80 percent of the time. Before he makes an investment, he is one of the most informed people on that product, service, company, or industry. Because of his wide-ranging research, he knows exactly what he is doing and exactly why he is doing it.

DAILY RITUALS

Most successful people have daily rituals that they follow. It is helpful for you to develop daily rituals as well. These are things you do automatically, over and over, which increase the probabilities that you will accomplish your goals.

For example, in general wealthy people take excellent care of their physical health. They go to bed early and get eight to nine hours of sleep each night. They often arise before 6:00 a.m., three hours before their first fixed appointment.

Successful people plan every day in advance. They make a list, usually the night before, of everything that they have to do the following day. They organize the list by priority, and select the most important thing they can do that day. Before they take on anything new, they write it down on their list and give it a priority.

This list gives them a track to run on and a tremendous sense of control over their days.

CONTINUALLY IMPROVE YOUR SKILLS

Top people build learning into each day. They read thirty to sixty minutes each morning—approximately one book per week. They read in areas that can be helpful to them in their work and search the Internet to continually alert themselves to new ideas and information in their particular fields.

▶ ▶ ▶

Top people build learning into each day.

Steve Jobs is famous for saying that "you can't be too attached to how you think your life is supposed to work out and instead trust that all the dots will be connected in the future."

Your job is to continually connect more dots. Learn more things. Gather more factoids— small pieces of information that can add detail to your picture—and give you new ideas and insights.

Your job is to continually collect more dots. Learn more things.

The difference between people in almost every field, the successful and the unsuccessful, is that the successful people simply "know more" than their competitors. They are better informed.

Subscribe to Summaries

Because you are busy, you should subscribe to and read book summaries. Use summary.com and getabstract.com to get the best ideas of the best business books coming out every month. Subscribe

to blinkist.com, an app that gives you fifteen minute summaries of top books, every week as well.

Listen to educational audio programs at every opportunity. Subscribe to audible.com, which has the best selection of educational audio programs in the world today. Download these programs onto your smartphone and listen to them whenever you get downtime—when you are driving, exercising, or walking and your mind is relaxed. Sometimes a single new idea, combined with your existing knowledge base, can be worth a fortune to you.

Take Additional Courses

Attend additional courses, seminars, and workshops. Go to lectures given by practical experts, people who are active and successful in the field on which they lecture. One seminar or workshop can give you ideas that can save you years of hard work trying to learn the same things on your own.

Take good notes when you are learning new things. A Chinese proverb says, "The palest ink is stronger than the most powerful memory." Record them on Evernote, a free app that is readily available. Then, review your notes on a regular basis.

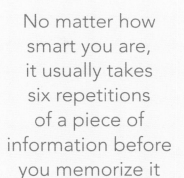

▶ ▶ ▶

No matter how smart you are, it usually takes six repetitions of a piece of information before you memorize it completely.

No matter how smart you are, it usually takes six repetitions of a piece of information before you memorize it completely. When you take notes, and review your notes regularly, you dramatically increase your level of retention, putting more ideas at your mental fingertips and making them available to you to improve your life and work.

GET SMARTER EVERY DAY

A journalist who worked for *Fortune* magazine for forty years recently retired. In their tribute to her, and her contributions to the magazine, they asked her

"I resolved to always go to bed at night smarter than when I woke up in the morning."

why she felt she had made such a difference over the years. She answered, "I resolved to always go to bed at night smarter than when I woke up in the morning."

You should do the same. Make it a ritual. Learn and practice something new each day. Increase the probabilities that you will be successful by increasing the number of dots that you have to connect with other dots to create new pictures and generate new ideas, enabling you to achieve greater goals. New ideas and insights can motivate you to get started and keep going until you succeed.

"Success is a consequence and must not be a goal."—Gustave Flaubert

CHAPTER SEVEN

NEVER

Give Up

> "There is no failure except in no longer trying. There is no defeat except from within, no really insurmountable barrier save our own inherent weakness of purpose."
> —*Elbert Hubbard*

I n 1895, Orison Swett Marden, founder of *Success* magazine and the author of *Pushing to the Front*, expressed one of the greatest success principles of all time. He said that there are two parts of success. The first is "get-to-itiveness," and the second is "stick-to-itiveness." My term for this approach is, "Get started and keep going."

Persistence and determination have always been the most important qualities for success. As hard as it is, almost anyone can get started. But to persevere through thick and thin, to continually pick yourself up again over and over, and face failure and disappointment, requires the best that is in you.

Napoleon Hill said, "Persistence is to the character of man as carbon is to steel."

The more you persist, the stronger you become. And the stronger you become, the more you are able to persist.

PERSISTENCE AND SELF-DISCIPLINE

There seems to be a direct relationship between persistence and self-discipline. The rule is that "persistence is self-discipline in action." It is when you force yourself to continue, discipline yourself to persist, when everything in you wants to give up that you develop the kind of character that will carry you over every obstacle.

Vince Lombardi said, "Quitters never win and winners never quit."

There is also a direct relationship between persistence and the qualities of self-esteem, self-respect, and personal pride. The more you discipline yourself to persist in the face of adversity, the more you will like and respect yourself, and the more powerful you will feel.

There is also a direct relationship between persistence and the qualities of self-esteem, self-respect, and personal pride.

Develop Persistence

Persistence is a habit, and like any habit you can develop it in yourself with practice and repetition. Every act of persistence and self-discipline strengthens every other act of persistence and self-discipline. Every failure of persistence and self-discipline weakens you in every other area as well. They are all interlinked.

Your subconscious mind is very powerful. You can actually preprogram it, like setting an alarm clock, to go off for you in the way you want it to. If you want to become a persistent person, you can program your mind in advance to never give up. The way you do this is simple—you simply say to yourself, "No matter what happens, I will never give up."

Surprisingly enough, your subconscious mind then accepts this as a command, just as if you had set a timer on your smartphone. Then, the next time you have a setback or disappointment that might cause an ordinary person to quit, your subconscious mind will "go off" and remind you, "You never give up." You'll actually find yourself saying "Wait a minute, I never give up."

YOU ARE IN CHARGE

Nelson Mandela said, "Do not judge me by my successes, judge me by how many times I fell down and got back up again."

There is only one person in the world who can stop you from

There is only one person in the world who can stop you from succeeding greatly, and that is yourself.

succeeding greatly, and that is yourself. If you resolve that you will never give up, persistence soon becomes an automatic response to any problem or adversity. Without even thinking about it, you pull yourself up, "suck it up," as they say, and keep moving forward.

Knowing how important persistence is to lifelong success, I practiced this "preprogramming" on my children as they were growing up. Throughout their young lives, I said the same thing to each one of them, over and over: "I know one thing about you. You never give up."

KEEP REPEATING THE MANTRA

No matter how many problems or difficulties they had, or how

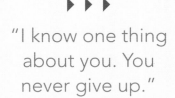

▶ ▶ ▶

"I know one thing about you. You never give up."

many times they were disappointed in themselves and their results, I would listen patiently and then say, "Well, I know one thing about you. You never give up."

And it worked. My children are now happy, healthy, self-confident adults, busy and active with their families and in their work, and they never give up. It is not a part of their world view. Quitting never occurs to them.

At a certain age, they took over their programming from me. Instead of my having to say "you never give up" to them on a regular basis, they simply began to say it to themselves. "No matter what happens, I never give up."

It is not part of their worldview. Quitting never occurs to them.

BECOMING UNSTOPPABLE

One of my seminar attendees once asked me what I thought was the most important quality for success in life. I thought about that for a while and then responded, "The quality of being unstoppable."

How do you become unstoppable?
You simply repeat the words "I am unstoppable!" to yourself, over and over. Then, no matter what happens, refuse to stop until you have achieved your goals.

Earlier, I said that a major turning point in my life was when I learned about goals. Shortly after that, I had a second turning point. It was when I discovered that you can learn any skill, quality, or habit that you want to learn to achieve any goal you can set for yourself. You can learn to be persistent, just like you can learn any subject. Wow!

THERE ARE NO LIMITS

You are not a human being, you are a human "becoming." You are constantly evolving and developing in the direction of your dominant thoughts. You can become anyone that you want to become, with any habits or skills that you want to develop. There

There are no limits except the limits you place on yourself.

are no limits except the limits you place on yourself.

When you decide to become a confident, competent, self-disciplined, and persistent person, and you practice and develop yourself every day, there are no limits to what you can be, have, and do in the exciting months and years ahead. You will confidently get started and keep going until you achieve the greatness for which you were born.

" **A winner** is someone who recognizes his God-given talents, works his tail off to develop them into

skills, and uses these skills

to accomplish his goals."

—Larry Bird

SUMMARY

A Great Time to
BE ALIVE

> "I will keep smiling, be positive, and never give up! I will give 100 percent each time I play. These are always my goals and my attitude."
>
> —*Yani Tseng*

This is a great time to be alive. There have never been more opportunities for more people to start new businesses, careers, and to succeed greatly than there are today.

The number of millionaires and billionaires is growing faster today than at any time in human history.

You have more natural talent and ability than you could use in one hundred lifetimes.

There is very little that you cannot accomplish if you are clear about your goals, develop written plans, and then work on them until you achieve them.

You are in complete charge of your own life. You are responsible. As a wise man said, "Don't go out and have a good day; instead, go out and make it a good day."

The secret of success has always been the same: get started and keep going.

If you can do these two things, every single day, there are no limits on what you can achieve.

JUST DO IT!

ABOUT THE AUTHOR

Brian Tracy is the chairman of Brian Tracy International, a human resources development company headquartered in Solana Beach, California. He has written seventy books and produced more than eight hundred audio and video training programs. His materials have been translated into forty-two languages and are used in sixty-four countries. He is active in community affairs and serves as a consultant to several nonprofit organizations.

Brian is also one of the top professional speakers and trainers in the world today. He addresses more than 250,000 men and women each year on the subjects of leadership, strategy, sales, personal achievement, and business success. He has given more than five thousand talks and seminars to five million people worldwide, bringing a unique blend of humor, insight, information, and inspiration to his audiences.

Brian lives with his wife, Barbara, and their four children in Solana Beach, California, and is an avid student of business, psychology, management, sales, history, economics, politics, metaphysics, and religion. He believes that each person has extraordinary untapped potential that he or she can learn to access and, in so doing, achieve more in a few years than the average person accomplishes in a lifetime.